Guidance for Change Management

My eyes established a vision for my life,

After seeing the beauty of Lord Shri Krishna (with belief, devotion and love).

My senses started working intelligently,

After understanding the morals of Lord Shri Krishna's stories and his past times (with belief, devotion and love).

My hands started writing good books,

After folding hands in front of Lord Shri Krishna (with belief, devotion and love).

Oh Lord Krishna, what am I without your blessing,

Oh Lord Krishna, your blessing is the reason for my breath, for my actions, for health, for prosperity, for peace and everything that I possess.

Hare Krishna Hare Krishna, Krishna Krishna Hare Hare,

Hare Rama Hare Rama, Rama Rama Hare Hare,

Table of contents

Register This Book

Thank you very much for purchasing this book.

First of all, before you read ahead, please **register your book** here:

https://servicemanagers.org/chm-registration

As a **ServiceManagers.Org ChM Book Club** member, you will receive lots of benefits and support from our Book Club Forum:

https://servicemanagers.org/chm-book-club

Certification Program

This is the official book for getting the **ServiceManagers.Org Certified Change Management Professional**™ (**ChMP**™) designation/credential program:

https://servicemanagers.org/chmp-certification

This Career Certification Program will improve your job opportunities and certify your skills gained from this book.

The Certification Exam is online, and once you sign up you can take it whenever you want (no deadline limits). Just sign up today for your exam, and start enjoying this book.

Preface

Today there are numerous books on ITSM, but none which tells how to implement and improve ITSM practices for organizations and how to bring effectiveness in ITSM operations. Hence, I have chosen to write books in this area, providing detailed information; this book "Guidance for Change Management" is part of a series with explicit focus on change management. The focus is on topics like implementing change management through Six Sigma's DMADV approach, improving change management through Six Sigma's DMAIC approach, Roles and responsibilities in change management, Essentials for change management operations, Integrations in change management with other processes and functions, and Interview questions for change management positions.

This book will be very useful for the beginners, experienced change analysts, change managers, change advisory board members, ITSM consultants, Service delivery managers, and ITSM process owners. In my opinion, the prerequisite for reading this book is that the reader should have already gotten certified in ITIL Foundation.

Next, this book has not been written just for the sake of writing 'while beating around the bush' on same topics with some flowery words just to increase the number of pages; the only intention I had, while writing the book, was to give knowledge which is not available on internet (for free).

Finally, if you are planning to gain in-depth knowledge on change management or aspiring to find a job in change management, this book is for you.

If this book interests you, you might also like other books published in the same series:

- Guidance for incident management
- Guidance for problem management

Acknowledgments

If I have to start thanking people name by name,

I should first thank my mother Krishna Kumari Pabbathi, for giving birth to me, with all the organs and body in good condition.

I should thank my father Surya Prakash Pabbathi, for teaching me the right morals, values, and placing me in one of the best school, sacrificing his comforts and pleasures.

I should thank my grandfather Satyanarayana Pabbathi, who iterated that good books are the greatest friends, and exemplified his life for principles.

I should thank Balasaraswathi Penmetsa, for teaching Mathematics patiently in my 10th class, when I was dumb at Mathematics, when no professional teacher could teach me with patience.

I should thank my graduation friend Venkatesham Padigela, who inspired me to become a topper in my graduation,

I should thank my friend Subba Rao, for helping me and supporting me in many instances of my life.

I should thank my first spiritual alma mater - ISKCON and my first spiritual mentor Kalakanta Prabhu, for making me understand life and Lord Krishna (which is the best thing that ever happened in all my life). Also my other mentors Srivasa Prabhu and Madan Sundar Prabhu who always show their mercy by giving great spiritual knowledge to me.

I know that I am still missing numerous people who have taught, helped, and supported me numerous times in my life.

Hence I would give my highest respects and surrender to the Supreme Lord Krishna for arranging all these wonderful people in my life, and giving me so many learning's, experiences and knowledge!!!

Big thanks to **Angel Berniz**, and **ServiceManagers.Org** for publishing another book.

About the author

Kiran Kumar Pabbathi has worked for various companies in the IT industry which gave him detailed insight of ITAM, ITSM, ITIL best practices and EAM.

Kiran has had the privilege to work in different roles taking care of service desk operations, request fulfillment, incident management, availability management, capacity management, information security management, IT service continuity management, sharepoint administration, project management, ITIL consulting and trainings, and ITAM Consulting.

Kiran is a certified professional in ITIL® Expert, PRINCE2® (Foundation and Practitioner), Six Sigma Green Belt, ISO/IEC20K – Foundation, Cloud Computing - Foundation, TMAP – Foundation (Test Management Professional), MCP in SharePoint 2003 Customizations, and MCTS in MS Project 2007. Kiran is also an accredited ITIL trainer and Invigilator for BCS, UK.

His other authoring works include:

- "PDCA for ITIL – Metrics, CSFs and workflows for implementing ITIL practices" published by TSO, UK (ISBN 9780117082076) which gives a direction for implementing ITIL processes and designing ITSM solutions.
- "Charm of friendship" published by Pothi, India (ISBN 9789382715924) explaining the importance of friendship for children.
- "Guidance for ITAM – Step by step implementation guide with workflows, metrics, best practices and checklists" published by ServiceManagers.Org (ISBN 9780991320509)

- "Guidance for EAM – Processes, implementation steps, workflows, best practices, and checklists" published by ServiceManagers.Org (ISBN 9780991320514)
- "Focus on IAM - CSFs, metrics, checklists, best practices, and guidelines for defining IAM processes and implementing IAM solutions" published by ServiceManagers.Org (ISBN 9780991320530)
- "Guidance for Incident Management - According to ISO/IEC 20000 & 9001 Standards, Six Sigma and ITSM Best Practices" published by ServiceManagers.Org (ISBN 9780991320547)
- "Guidance for Problem Management - According to ISO/IEC 20000 & 9001 Standards, Six Sigma and ITSM Best Practices" published by ServiceManagers.Org (ISBN 9780991320554)

Introduction to Change Management

Basic Terminology

Back-out Plan: Plan that details the steps to restore the service or CI to its original condition; it is for when a planned change does not deliver expected results.

Best Practices: Practices that are well recognized and which have proved the ability for demonstrating success in respective areas (e.g.: PMBOK for project management, ITIL for IT service management, MOF for IT service management, COBIT for IT governance, etc.).

Capability: Any intangible assets like processes, knowledge used in managing an application, IT service, or other configuration item (CI).

Change: Any addition or modification or removal of a CI and its attributes in the live environment.

Change Advisory Board (CAB): Committee of representatives to validate and approve change requests based on a business justification.

Change Category: A structure that organizes a group of similar types of changes.

Change Implementation Plan: Plan that details the complete coverage on change implementation explaining who should own the change, who will implement the change, who will test the change, what are the prerequisites for implementing change, how the change has to be implemented, definition of back out plan, definition of remediation plan, etc.

Change Management: Change management defines a standardized process for registering, categorizing, evaluating, and approving the changes.

Change Model: Change model is a predefined workflow that is followed for regular and routine kinds of changes. It defines a repeatable way of dealing with a particular category of change.

Change Record: A record that contains the complete details of a change from the RFC stage to the closure phase.

Conflicting Change: A change that is conflicting or colliding with another scheduled change on a same CI.

Critical Success Factor (CSF): Vital principles necessary for the success of a business; it is based on CSFs and metrics are developed.

DFSS/DMADV: A systematic methodology defined in six sigma philosophy to design products and processes which can meet customer expectations.

DMAIC: A systematic methodology defined in six sigma philosophy for continuous process improvement.

Emergency Change: Any change that is implemented to restore a service or to avoid an outage of a service, especially when it impacts multiple users. Emergency changes would need emergency CAB approvals to validate and approve the change.

Event: Any occurrence/observation that has significance to the delivery of IT services. Events are notifications that are received through email/mobile devices created by IT service, configuration device, or monitoring tools.

Expedite Change: Any change that has to be implemented as soon as possible due to a business need but not relating to an incident.

Forward Schedule of Changes (FSC): Schedule that contains details of upcoming changes. Also called change schedule.

Impact: Measure that defines the number of users affected by an outage. Usually denoted as 1,2,3,4.

Incident: Any unplanned breakdown or reduction in quality of IT service delivered by a service provider is called an incident.

IT Infrastructure: It is the collection of hardware, software, and people-ware in an IT organization.

ITSM (Information Technology Service Management): Management of IT services to meet the organization's business goals.

Key Performance Indicator (KPI): Vital metrics necessary for an organization to meet its business goals, which reflect the CSFs of an organization.

Mean Time Between Failures (MTBF): Metric that defines the average time that a CI or IT Service can operate its agreed function without any breakdown.

Mean time between system incidents (MTBSI): MTBSI is the mean time from when an IT Service fails, until it next fails. MTBSI can be derived through the formula, MTBSI = MTBF + MTRS.

Mean Time to Repair (MTTR): Average time taken to repair a CI or service after an outage.

Mean Time to Restore Service: Average time taken to restore a CI or service after an outage.

Metric: Measurements that quantitatively evaluate the performance of IT operations.

Normal Change: Changes that carry significant amount of risk and which are new, discrete, and unique to IT infrastructure. Normal changes would relatively take more time than standard and emergency changes; they would also need CAB and technical CAB approvals to verify and validate a change.

Policy: Policy is a management directive that significantly influences processes and procedures.

Proactive Change Management: Activity in change management which focuses on ensuring the change requests are well planned, registered, categorized, assessed, tested, and approved as per the change management process.

Priority: Measure used to identify the criticality of an incident/problem/change. Usually denoted as 1, 2, 3, and 4. Calculated through the formula, Priority= (Impact + Urgency)/2

Problem: Unknown underlying root cause of one or more incidents.

Process: A set or sequence of activities that results in achieving an output or business goal.

Reactive Change Management: Activity in change management which focuses on the changes requests that have failed, backed out, rolled back, and remediated;

accordingly, the RCA is performed why deviations/ discrepancies have occurred.

Remediation Plan: Plan that details the alternative steps to be followed to minimize risk when a planned change does not deliver expected results.

Request For Change (RFC): Request created by the users or IT staff, capturing the details of a requested change.

Resources: Any tangible assets (like IT infrastructure, people, money, or anything) that will be helpful to deliver an IT service.

Sigma: It is a Greek letter representing a statistical unit of measurement that defines the standard deviation of a population, which measures the variability or spread of the data.

Six Sigma: An approach to improve the process quality by eliminating defects and minimizing variability.

Service: Provision of value to customers without any ownership of risks and internal costs associated in developing a service.

Standard: Rules and conventions that help to implement policies and enforce required conventions.

Standard Change: Changes that are low in risk and which can be implemented by following a predefined model. Standard changes are pre-approved, pre-authorized, and they have a predefined workflow.

Transition: The ability to handover services from build stage to operational environment.

Urgency: Measure that defines how soon the service has to be restored. It is usually denoted as 1,2,3,4.

Validation: Activity that validates the deployed change to check whether or not it meets the customer's expectations.

Verification: Activity that verifies the deployed change to ensure that it is working without any defects.

Objectives of Change Management

- To define standard process and procedures for managing changes (which includes registering, categorizing, evaluating, and approving) in IT infrastructure.
- Mitigate risks associated with a change.
- Ensure that the changes bring value to IT and business departments.

Objectives of DMAIC and DMADV

- To define effective and efficient processes.
- To improve the consistency and efficiency of processes.
- To improve customer satisfaction and reduce the operational costs.
- To solve issues and reduce the variation.

Change management in real IT operations

Change management in real IT operations starts with a change request or RFC logged by an ITSM or IT stakeholder such as an incident/problem/availability/capacity management team member, etc.

For example:

An incident management team member can raise a RFC when he/she has to fix some issue with respect to an emergency change.

A problem management team member can raise a RFC when he/she has developed a permanent fix (to a problem ticket) which needs to be deployed in the IT infrastructure.

An availability/capacity management team member can raise a RFC when he/she identifies an issue with respect to availability/capacity.

An information security management team member can raise a RFC to change a security policy or procedure or to change an access control mechanism.

Examples:

1) In infrastructure environment, addition of 2TB RAM to a server.
2) In application management support, addition of a new functionality in an application or restarting an application server.

Activities in change management

- A change request is logged or raised by an ITSM stakeholder who can be called a change requestor.
- Change analyst validates the detailed description provided by the change requestor.
- Change analyst prioritizes the change request based on the inputs.
- Change analyst categorizes the changes like major/ minor or standard/normal/emergency/expedite as per the organizational policies.
- Change analyst performs the impact and risk analysis.
- Change analyst creates and assigns the change tasks for different technical teams (who will have to complete the tasks, it can be anyone like DEV/UAT)
- Change analyst provides the information update to the change requestor with information on:

  RFC number

  Target date and time

  Change tasks number
- Change analyst ensures the detailed implementation plans are updated in every change task.
- Change analyst ensures a back-out plan and remediation plan is updated for the planned change.
- Change analyst verifies that every change request is updated with all the necessary information as per the policies.
- RFC is presented to the CAB/ECAB
- CAB/ECAB approve or reject the change request in the change management tool.

- Change analyst triggers the Release and deployment management process through a release ticket.
- Change manager is accountable for the change management activities and ensures all these activities are done as per policies and procedures.
- Release and deployment management team members do the release planning, building, testing, and deployment plans with respect to schedules.
- Release and deployment management team defines the training plans and ELS (Early Life Support) for the new releases.
- Release and deployment management team deploys the releases ensuring there are no release collisions happening.
- The change/release requests are closed before the SLA breaches.
- Finally, all change and release teams together perform a post implementation review to check if everything went fine as per the process & procedures.

Roles and Responsibilities in Change management

Change Manager

Change Manager manages the change management team and ensures that the change operations are executed as per the defined processes, procedures, and SLAs. This role's main objective is to minimize the risks and adverse impacts of changes (to IT environment) and also provides the subject matter expertise on reviewing the business case and approved change requests/RFCs.

Responsibilities of Change Manager

- Maintaining change management system, including policies, processes, systems, metrics and procedures that are used across the entire IT business and adheres to all regulatory requirements.
- Research & proactively identify opportunities to process, measurements, and systems in order to improve the effectiveness and efficiency of change management services.
- Work closely and communicate effectively with users and stakeholders of the change process to drive the improvements.
- Assure service quality objectives, governance compliance, and responsiveness through KPIs and metrics.
- Attends all CAB meetings.
- Support the development and execution change management activities in partnership with customer teams - including stakeholder engagement, communication, training, and readiness and adoption measurement plans.

- Collaborate with the team and key stakeholders to ensure timely delivery and quality of assigned deliverables.
- Identify possible issues/concerns, escalate risks and issues to management and project leadership teams, and implement mitigation plans if necessary.
- Identify training needs by analysis of common errors.
- Keep the customers and internal stakeholders up to date on high priority changes through timely and regular written and verbal communications.
- Review the business case of all RFCs/change requests and formulate a plan of action for handling the change based on area of expertise/responsibility.
- Ensure change management documentation is updated.
- Gather and analyze information on a variety of changes and develop action plans to contain and control incidents.
- Liaison with internal training and communications staff to produce user guidance and bulletins explaining best practice and common issues.
- Provide information and reports on change implementations, successful changes, and failed changes.
- Verify implemented changes.
- Conduct PIR on successful and failed changes and conduct RCA.

Note: Responsibilities can differ based on organization's requirements.

Required qualifications and skill set

Technical skills:

- Working experience and good knowledge of change management methodologies like:
    1. Leavitt's system model
    2. Burke-Litwin change model
    3. Kotter's 8 step change model

- Thorough understanding and knowledge on project planning and risk management for IT systems.
- Hands-on experience of enterprise IT systems with respect to databases, servers, and other IT components.
- Knowledge of concepts and philosophies regarding the design and deployment of information technologies and associated architectural concepts, principles and tools.
- Ability to understand the basic tenets of the physical IT system and that system's relation to the application.
- Experienced in multiple aspects of IT operations.

Must have:

- A bachelor's degree in computer science or a related discipline.
- Extensive experience in all aspects of network, virtualization, cloud issues, and stakeholder management.
- Few years of experience in change management.
- ITIL v3 Intermediate certification in Service Transition.
- Excellent communication, documentation and presentation skills.

- Ability to negotiate, plan and, communicate change activities across the organization.
- Good analytical and systematic approach to problem solving.
- Excellent judgment, tact, and decision-making ability.
- Solid understanding of foundational IT technical issues and relationships.

Recommended skills:

- Thorough knowledge on project management methodologies.
- Knowledge on quality assurance and audits.

  Note: Required skills can differ based on organization's requirements.

Change Analyst

Change analyst handles and manages the change management operational activities which involves registering, categorizing, reviewing, planning, and preparing necessary documentation for the change requests.

Responsibilities of Change Analyst

- Register, categorize, and prioritize changes after conducting thorough analysis
- Conduct risk analysis before submitting it for CAB approval
- Facilitate CAB meetings
- Maintain a balance between the business need for prompt change and the necessity of ensuring that stability of existing systems is not compromised.
- Document and publish the CAB - MOM (Minutes of the meetings)
- Reroute misdirected changes that have not been handled in a timely manner
- Identify changes that needs special attention or escalation
- Ensure change report is created immediately after successful implementation
- Draft and send out communications to ensure that all relevant stakeholders are aware of procedures

- Work with change manager to ensure change activities are properly communicated
- Ensure change implementers are adhering to the process and procedures as defined

  Note: Responsibilities can differ based on organization's requirements.

Required qualifications and skill set

Technical skills:

- Good understanding on IT systems and environments
- Ability to ensure that the defined process and procedures are followed
- Proven experience of working in change management operations

Must have:

- A bachelor's degree in computer science or a related discipline.
- Excellent written and verbal skills
- Proven experience in the use of MS Office products
- Experience in working with remote teams
- Attitude to work in a complex IT environment
- Ability to prioritize busy workload

  Note: Required skills can differ based on organization's requirements.

Change Advisory Board (CAB) members

Change advisory board members should be very knowledgeable in change management process and specific technology and domains. They will have the decision making authority to approve or reject a change request/ RFC. CAB members discuss whether or not a RFC should be approved or rejected at CAB meetings.

Responsibilities of CAB

- Responsible for making accurate and effective decisions on whether or not the RFC would bring positive results, value to the organization, reduce the manual efforts, and reduce the costs.
- Approve changes/reject the changes based on:
  1. the risk to IT services and business services
  2. impact of a change on availability, performance, security, compliance, and SLAs
  3. provision of procedures
  4. test plans defined
  5. test results gathered
- Ensure that the change is planned well and is equipped with all procedures to test and implement.
- Review the implemented changes

- Discuss previously failed, rolled back, and backed out changes to understand what went wrong

  Note: Responsibilities can differ based on organization's requirements.

Required qualifications and skill set

Technical skills:

- ITIL v3 intermediate service transition
- Six sigma black belt certification
- Knowledge in performing RCA (Root Cause Analysis)
- Work experience in different ITSM processes and strong experience in change management operations.

Must have:

- A bachelor's degree in computer science or a related discipline.
- Excellent written and verbal skills.
- Excellent customer facing skills with experience of working with remote teams.
- Attitude to work in a complex IT environment.
- Excellent communication with experience of a global organization.
- Knowledge and understanding of enterprise IT systems.

  Note: Required skills can differ based on organization's requirements.

Essentials for Change Management Operations

Metrics for change management operations

Metrics for change management operations are essential ingredients that assess and evaluate the performance of operational activities and will stand as a basis for improvement of change management operations.

Metrics for change management operations can be described as below:

- Total number of changes (including emergency changes, standard changes, and normal changes)
- Total number of unauthorized and unapproved changes (for emergency changes and normal changes)
- Total number of successful changes (with respect to emergency changes, standard changes, and normal changes)
- Total number of failed changes (with respect to emergency changes, standard changes, and normal changes)
- Total number of changes that were backed out (with respect to emergency changes, standard changes and normal changes)
- Total costs involved in change implementations (with respect to emergency changes, standard changes, and normal changes)
- Total number of emergency changes
- Average time needed for implementing an emergency change
- Number of successful emergency changes
- Number of failed emergency changes
- Number of emergency changes that were backed out

- Number of unauthorized emergency changes
- Average time taken for emergency change approval
- Total number of standard changes
- Average time needed for implementing a standard change
- Number of successful standard changes
- Number of failed standard changes
- Number of standard changes that were backed out
- Number of unauthorized standard changes
- Average time taken for standard change approval
- Total number of normal changes
- Average time needed for implementing a normal change
- Number of successful normal changes
- Number of failed normal changes
- Number of unauthorized normal changes
- Number of normal changes that were backed out
- Average time taken for normal change approval
- Number of major changes
- Number of minor changes
- Number of changes that were not completed on time
- Number of changes that were not completed in budget
- Average Csat % on a change
- Size of change backlog
- Change management staff utilization rate
- Number of Emergency CAB staff
- Number of Technical CAB staff
- Total team size of change management operations
- Number of CAB meetings organized per a change
- Number of training sessions organized for a change management operations staff
- Number of incidents raised due to a change
- Number of changes which met customer requirements

Metrics for change management process

Metrics for change management process are essential ingredients that assess and evaluate the defined process and its implementation, and it will stand as the basis for improvement of process.

Metrics for change management process can be described as below:

- Time taken to develop change management process and its collaterals
- Number of resources and man days required for process development
- Number of resources and man days required for process testing
- Number of resources and man days required for process collaterals editing
- Number of technical discrepancies found in all process collaterals
- Number of linguistic discrepancies (typos, confusions, grammatical errors) found in process documentation
- Number of defects found by end users and customer teams in collaterals
- Number of documentation deliverables (process guides, standard operating procedures, work instructions, role & responsibilities) available on a process
- Number of NCs (Non-conformances) found in audits with respect to process
- Number of areas where there is no documentation available
- Number of process training sessions provided

- Customer satisfaction rating on process documentation provided
- Customer satisfaction rating on process training sessions and trainer

Best practices for change management

Best practices are those real practices that have delivered efficient, effective, and excellent results in the IT processes and real operations.

Best practices for change management processes and operations can be defined as mentioned below:

- **Define a CAB team for evaluating and approving every change**

  There should be a defined ECAB team giving explicit and meticulous focus on understanding the emergency change (its impact and associated services), evaluating the risks, verifying the back out and remediation plan, and approving/rejecting with respect to business justification.

  There should be a defined CAB team giving explicit and meticulous focus on understanding the normal changes (its impact and associated services), evaluating the risks, verifying the back out and remediation plan, and approving/rejecting with respect to business justification.

  There should also be a TCAB & DCAB team giving explicit and meticulous focus on all changes to evaluate the technical and deployment aspects and risks in every change request/RFC logged.

- **Change planning is a must for every normal and emergency change**

  Change analysts should do appropriate planning, before the RFCs/Change requests are sent for approvals and evaluation to avoid wastage of time and efforts. Planning should normally analyze and make a log of:

1. What is the reason for change and how many incidents/problems are associated with it?
2. What is the return from the change?
3. What are the risks involved?
4. What are the resources needed?
5. What will be the impact on other services?
6. What CIs are involved in the change?
7. What is the relationship between the CIs involved in a change to other services?
8. What is the priority?
9. What will be the appropriate date and time?

- **Irrespective of urgency on the RFC, testing on change should never be skipped**
  Adequate testing on changes is a mandatory activity that should happen without a miss. All the testing work should happen on the test environment which should be exactly the same like the operational environment.
  Untested change can lead to very serious incidents/problems bringing disruption to IT service, penalization, and SLA breaches.

- **Maintenance of change records for all normal changes and emergency changes**
  All the details of changes throughout the lifecycle (RFC details, categorization, risk assessments done, approval log, procedures followed, back out plan, remediation plan, and PIR log) should be captured and documented in change records which will be helpful for future references to operational and management staff.

- **Define control procedures for managing change tickets**
  Definition of control procedures for managing change tickets should be must, like:
  1. Closed change ticket cannot be reopened.
  2. Priority of a change ticket cannot be increased/reduced unless there is a business justification.

- **Control on emergency changes**
  Change manager should always strive to curb the emergency changes as most of the unexpected issues/discrepancies happen in emergency changes (due to a lack of planning).

- **No changes can be approved without back out plan**
  Back out plan will play a very important role in change implementation as this plan documents step by step procedure for any change analyst to bring the service/ CI to the baseline (to its original and accepted position).

- **Definition of change models for routine issues**
  Change models defines pre-defined steps for handling particular types of change that are routine which can save great time and effort for the change management staff.
- **Documentation of lessons learned**
  Documentation of lessons learned should be a must, and should be submitted as knowledge articles to verify and validate them and to publish them in knowledge base.

- **Implementation of authorized and approved changes**
  Unauthorized and unapproved changes should never be implemented in a production environment; it is very

possible that there would be tight schedules, SLAs, and follow ups from customers but yet no policies and procedures can be ignored.

- **Have a unified calendar with complete visibility**
  Having an integrated calendar accessible to change, release, and other operational teams like incident and problem would be very helpful to see planned changes and releases by time, day, week and month.

- **Participation of change management staff in service improvement meetings**
  Participation of change staff in service improvement meetings is very vital to understand the priorities and goals of IT organization and accordingly change management staff should align its operations. Also change staff can provide many great inputs for improving the IT service delivery.

- **Regular meetings with other ITSM process owners**
  Regular meetings with other ITSM process owners should happen continuously to update the trends and patterns of RFCs and the concerns of EU's and customers.

- **Maintenance of ITSM process owners and onsite technicians contacts list**
  Maintenance of ITSM process owners, onsite technicians and service owner's contacts details, and being up to date is a must which will enable the change management staff to do the planning & coordination with other service transition stakeholders.

CSFs

- **Selection of right human resources**
  Selection of right human resources with good experience in change management operations, technical knowledge, analytical skills, communication skills and customer service attitude is a must for change management staff; it can be ranked as a number one issue among all the CSFs in change management.

- **Clarity in roles and responsibilities**
  Establishing clear roles and responsibilities for the Change Advisory Board (CAB), Change Manager, Change implementer, and Change Analysts is very vital for efficient operations.

- **Develop an effective process before buying a tool**
  No tools in the market would make a perfect match for your business requirements. Hence, it is very essential to develop the process understanding the inputs, outcomes, activities, roles, risks, interfaces, dependencies (based on your requirements) and then select/build a tool with respect to the process.

- **Clearly defined scope**
  There should be a clear definition of scope concerning what change management team can handle and what is out of scope, which will in turn reduce the burden on change management staff eliminating the unnecessary efforts and time on registering and reviewing RFCs which are out of scope.

- **Regular training sessions**
  Training sessions on change management process, policies, procedures and technical knowledge is a must which should happen at regular intervals.
  Most of the delays and discrepancies in change management operations happen due to unawareness on process, policies, and procedures; hence, it is a mandatory objective for IT management to conduct training sessions which can bring thorough awareness to all stakeholders. Management should also conduct exams and assessments to evaluate the proficiency of the staff, and reward them with some gifts or incentives.

- **Thorough understanding of SLAs, OLAs and UCs**
  Unawareness on the SLAs, OLAs and UCs causes most of the penalizations and SLA breaches. Hence, management should make a conscious effort to make adequate awareness of SLAs, OLAs and UCs for all services through training sessions, posters, etc.

- **Integrated ITSM tool that can accommodate all ITSM process activities and functions**
  Management should select and deploy an integrated ITSM tool which can accommodate all ITSM processes and functions; having separate tools for different processes will increase burden (in terms of human resources efforts) and complexity (in terms of technology to do explicit integration).

- **Selection of right ITSM tool**
  Selection of the right ITSM tool which can fit your business requirements, which can be single point of contact for all your ITSM processes in your organization, which follows the ITSM terminology and best practices, which has decision making, reporting and data mining capabilities, and which is easy to use should be an ideal tool.

- **Access to KEDB, CMDB, CMS and SKMS**
  Change management staff should have access to KEDB, CMDB, CMS and SKMS; accessibility to these tools will help the staff to understand the impact of a change, associated services, SLAs associated, financial value, etc. and will help them to evaluate the risks associated.

- **Definition of a database for all successfully implemented changes**
  Definition of a database/repository which stores all change records (which encapsulates all change information), change models, plans and procedures at one place, will enable the key stakeholders to make effective decisions on change operations.

Checklist for change management team members

Checklists for change management operational staff will be helpful to consolidate the complete details of a change request. These questions can be mentioned as below:

- Who raised the change?
- Who will be affected by the change?
- What assets are the targets of the proposed change (servers, applications, network, etc.)?
- What is the change timeline?
- Are any other planned changes affected by this change?
- How much will this change cost?
- Are there times when this change should be avoided (month end, yearend, weekend, overnight)?
- Who should own this change?
- Who will perform this change (change implementers)?
- Is training required to perform this change?
- What is the priority of the change based on associated risk and urgency?
- What is the business or technical reason for the change?
- Who will be affected by the change if it fails?
- Can we test the change, before it touches the live environment?
- What will happen if the change is not implemented?
- How successful were similar changes in the past?
- What is the rollback plan if the change should fail?
- What is the remediation plan defined for the change?
- What will be the worst case service outage be?

- Is any SLA target affected by the change?
- What is the scheduled date?
- When will the change be performed and when will it be completed?
- When will the benefits of the change be realized (Immediately, Within a Month, Increasing benefits over a period of time)?
- How will issues be escalated?
- What is the rollback plan if the change should fail?
- What will a successful change look like when implemented?
- What IT services needs to be verified after making the change?
- What are the feedbacks received from PIR?

Checklist for CABs and change manager:

- Is there a change plan which includes business justification, risks, issues, design plan, test plan, and implementation procedures?
- Is there a defined rollback plan and is it tested?
- Is there a defined remediation plan and is it tested?
- What will a successful change look like when implemented?
- Who will perform this change (change implementers)?
- Is training required to perform this change?
- What is the priority of the change based on associated risk and urgency? Is the assessment done correctly?
- What is the business or technical reason for the change?
- Who will be affected by the change if it fails?
- What are the risks associated with a change? Is there a mitigation plan? Does it work well?

- Is there any supporting documentation prepared for implementing the change?
- Is the change scheduled appropriately in the FSC, ensuring major changes are first implemented?

Checklist for major changes

- Have you created a clear business case for change (including budget, time duration, resource, quality plan and acceptance criteria), identifying why the status quo is no longer appropriate?
- Have you assessed 'readiness for change' identifying the forces supporting change such as sponsorship, culture of continuous improvement, etc.?
- Have you completed an analysis of all the stakeholders and identified appropriate management strategies to address their needs and concerns?
- Have you identified direct and indirect impacts of the change e.g. to IT systems, facilities and accommodation, budgets, timing of other programs and services, start dates for changes and new staff, and responded with appropriate plans to address these impacts?
- Have you identified the type and nature of the communications required while implementing the change?
- Have you identified, informed, and engaged all the appropriate parties you need to collaborate with in order to implement the change and all the stakeholders impacted by the change?
- Have you determined if the staff has appropriate skills to implement the change?

- Do you have the test environment defined which is the same like operational/production environment?
- Have you conducted functionality, performance, usability, reliability, and security testing?

Checklists for assessing change management process

Assessment checklist for Change management process will be helpful for Change management operational staff to understand how effectively the process has been defined. This checklist can also be used by a quality team to evaluate the effectiveness of process and operations. This assessment checklist can be described as below:

- Do you develop a business case before implementing any major changes?
- Do you assess 'readiness for change' identifying the forces supporting change such as sponsorship, stakeholders interest, etc.?
- Do you have defined goals and objectives for change management; is the change management staff aware of the goals and objectives?
- Do you have a defined scope for change management process; is the change management staff aware of it?
- Do you have defined Policies, Principles, and Procedures for handling all types of changes?
- Do you have defined timescales for handling all changes?
- Do you have predefined change models; are they effective in delivering results?
- Do you create change records for all normal and emergency changes?
- Is there a definition of triggers, inputs, outputs, and interfaces made for change management process?
- Do you identify the direct and indirect impacts of the change?

- Do you identify what type of communication is required while implementing the change?
- Do you keep the staff informed of the vision for the change, the status and progress of the change process and where they can get more information and support?
- Do you execute change management operations responding to staff input, providing an explanation of what suggestions will be acted on and why some actions can't be taken?
- Are you helping staff keep perspective of what is 'business as usual' which can provide a base of the known and familiar whilst other things change?
- Do you provide timely and accurate feedback on the implementation process?
- Do you have procedures defined to provide additional resources if required, reallocating or reprioritizing work and resources?
- Do you inform the stakeholders on how the change will make a difference after implementation?
- Do you inform the stakeholders on how the change is making a difference?
- Do you conduct a change evaluation from stakeholders?
- Do you have defined CSFs, KPIs and metrics?
- Do you define the challenges and risks for every RFC?
- Do you get enough training sessions on process and technology to keep your staff with updated knowledge?
- Do you have a well-defined knowledge base, CMS, CMDB's? Do you find any errors or discrepancies in the knowledge articles (in these databases)?
- Can you relate your incident records and problem records with a change request/ RFC in the ITSM tool?
- Is your staff having access to CMS and CMDB's?

- Do you conduct any assessments or evaluation methods to check the knowledge of your staff?
- Are all your changes managed and stored in a single management system?
- Does your change and release tickets follow the same classification schema with respect to CTI?
- Do you make a log on lessons learnt, and is it stored in the database?
- Do you perform PIRs, after implementing a change?
- Do you conduct any audits on change records, to ensure that all the details are entered and categorized correctly?

Ticket auditing on change tickets

Ticket auditing on change tickets will evaluate the effectiveness and quality of change management practices and operations. It ensures that change tickets are appropriately categorized, adequately documented, prioritized, approved, assigned, and closed.

Some of the important parameters that have to be verified in change tickets are:

- Brief description of the change ticket; also ensure that the change description is not changed till the change closure
- Categorization of the change ticket, if it has been done appropriately (like standard change, normal change, emergency change); also ensure that categorized change is not modified from standard change to normal change.
- Categories of changes match with descriptions.
- Change assignments are done appropriately.
- Change interlinking (release/ problem/ etc.) is done appropriately.
- CAB reviews and justifications are documented.
- Change implementation start date and end date is followed correctly.
- Ensure all change tasks are updated with accurate information.

- Ensure every change request has a defined back-out plan.
- Ensure PIR is conducted for all normal changes, emergency changes, and failed changes.

Provision of channels to change management tools and other ITSM tools and databases

Change management tools and Service asset and configuration management tools and databases

Provision of channels to CMDB and CMS with change management tools would be helpful for the change management staff to:

- plan the changes accurately by identifying and understanding the underlying CIs and its relationship with other CIs.

- identify the number of changes/releases, incidents, and problems associated with the service and will help them to make quicker and effective decisions to carry out the operations.

Change management tools and Release and deployment management tools and databases

Provision of channels to release management tools and databases with change management tools would help the staff to:

- do appropriate follow up on the approved changes.
- check the release plans developed.

And will help them to ensure better insight on release deployments.

Change management tools and financial management tools and databases

Provision of channels to financial management databases with change management is not necessary. But you can provide channels/access for Change managers and CABs to financial management databases to understand the financial value associated with a change.

Change management tools and Service level management tools and databases

Provision of channels to SLM databases with change management tools would help the staff to:

- identify and understand the SLAs associated with a service.
- identify and understand the SLAs for an incident/problem and do the respective change plans.

And will help them to make quicker and effective decisions to carry out the operations.

Change management tools and Service Validation and Testing tools and databases

Provision of channels to SVT tools and databases with change management tools would enable the change staff to:

- check the test plans defined, and validate if they really cover all the scenarios.
- identify the defects logged by SVT.

Change management tools and Continual Service Improvement tools and databases

Provision of channels to CSI databases with change management tools would enable the change staff to:

- Document new recommendations to improve services.
- Identify improvement opportunities with respect to trends in operations.

Important details to be captured in Change tickets and reports

Important details to be captured in Change tickets and reports are:

Change Number: a unique ID registered for the change

Change Description: the description of the change

Change Location: the location where the change will be implemented

Change Requester: the person who requested the change request/RFC

Change Analyst: the name of the change analyst who has analyzed the change request/RFC

Change Requested Date: the date on which the change was requested

Change Triggered By: defines the sources that triggered the change like legal requirements, business requirements, etc.

Change Classification: the classification of the change like Normal, Standard, and Emergency

Category: the category of the change (Check the CTI structure mentioned in this book)

Type: the type of change (Check the CTI structure mentioned in this book)

Item: item of the change (Check the CTI structure mentioned in this book)

Risk analysis: describes the risks associated with the change

Business Case: the plan which defines the business justification, benefits, and resources needed

Rollback Plan: the description of the rollback plan

Remediation Plan: the description of the remediation plan

Impacting Services: the services that will be impacted by the change

Impacting CIs: the CIs that will be impacted by the change

Relative Benefit of Implementing the Change: the benefit of implementing change

Relative Cost: This should define the relative costs

Estimated Effort in Man Days or Hours: Man days or hours

Change Approval/Rejected Date: the date and time when the change was approved/ rejected by CAB

CAB Decision: a decision made by the CAB

CAB Comments: comments given by the CAB

ECAB Decision: decision made by the ECAB

ECAB comments: comments given by the ECAB

Change Manager: name of the change manager

Impact: The number of people that will be affected by change

Urgency: how soon the change has to be implemented

Priority: It will be based on impact and urgency

SLAs Associated: SLAs associated with change management

SLA Target Date and Time: date and time when the SLAs will be breached with respect to the change

Major Change Review: This determines if it's a major change

Major Change Justification: This defines the business justification and why it should be treated as a major change

Associated Changes: other change tickets that are associated with this change

Associated Incidents: the details of the incident tickets that are associated with this change

Associated Incidents: the details of the problem tickets that are associated with this change

SLAs Breach Details: the description why the SLAs were breached, and by how many minutes or hours did we breach the SLAs.

Sample RFC template

Sample RFC template (for teams who manage the RFCs manually) with some important details as described below:

REQUEST FOR CHANGE				
RFC No		Status		Request Date
Requester		email		
Nature of Change		Change Location		
Job Category		Change Category		
Title of the Change				
Why the change is required				
CAB Meeting Held		CAB MoM		
Any fault ticket no. before change		Customers / Business affected		
Change Implementer Details				
Name		email		
Dept		Workgroup		
Contact No		Position		
Proposed Start Date & Time		Proposed End Date & Time		
Duration		Predefined change duration		
Reason for asking more time				
Estimated outage details		Cause min outage		
		Min outage start		
Predefined min outage duration		Min outage end		
Minimum outage details				
Worst case duration		Worst case outage details		
Change requester Manager	Approved By		Approved Date & Time	
Change Confirmation	Actual start Date & Time		Actual end Date and Time	
	Actual outage start		Actual outage end	
Change Management Team official Use:-				
Change request closed date		Closed By		
Remarks				

Risk analysis on RFCs

As we all know change is any addition/ modification/ deletion of a CI or CI attribute in IT operational environment; so obviously whenever there is a change being made, it would definitely have some risk associated.

Hence, risk analysis is a must for every change, and this activity allows the change management team to identify, categorize, prioritize, and mitigate or avoid the risks. Hence, here is a template for conducting the risk analysis on changes as mentioned below:

- **Risk Name:** name of the risk such as server unavailability/slow performance/access without authentication
- **Description:** a detailed description of the risk
- Type: type of risk that can be classified as major, normal, minor, etc.
- **Priority:** Priority can be denoted as 1,2,3,4.
- **Classification:** Classification can be done as financial, hazard, operational, etc.
- **Relationship to Other Risks:** This should define the relationships with other risks.
- **Scope of Services:** This should define the scope of services where the risk can have an impact.
- **Impact on Stakeholders:** This should define the impact with respect to internal/external stakeholders.

- **Likelihood:** This should define the level of likelihood which can be described as "low", "medium", and "high".
- **Severity:** This should define the level of severity which can be described as "low", "medium", or "high" based on the number of users affected.
- **Response:** This should define the approach that will be used to avoid/mitigate/transfer the risk.
- **Response Actions:** This should define the actions that will be taken to deal with the risk.
- **Risk Analysis Team:** team members who have worked on this change.
- **Analysis Time Duration:** This should define the time spent on analyzing the risks
- **Residual Likelihood:** This should define the likelihood of the risk being realized once the risk response actions are carried out.
- **Residual Impact:** This should define the impact of the risk being realized once the risk response actions are carried out.
- **Residual Risk Score:** This should define the final residual risk score, and is a calculated value by weighting and multiplying values for residual likelihood and impact. Compare the residual risk score against the inherent risk score to determine if the response will be effective.

Change coordination

Change coordination is an activity which ensures that change requests/RFCs are well planned, registered, categorized, assessed, tested, approved and closed as per the agreed process and procedures.

Activities carried out by change coordinators can be described as:

- Validation of the information provided by Change Requestor.
- Prioritization of the change ticket based on the information provided.
- Informing the requestor about the change request number, priority, planned date, etc.
- Informing the change manager and contacting SMEs to define the implementation plan, back-out plan, rollback plan, remediation plans, etc.
- Informing the teams about the target date and time.
- Conducting pre-implementation meetings before sending the change requests for approvals.
- Ensuring no change collisions happen.
- Present all the change requests in CAB, and ensure all the approvals are done like TCAB, DCAB, etc.

- Trigger the release and deployment management process for making the change move into production environment.
- Liaise with necessary stakeholders to coordinate change building, testing, and implementation in accordance with schedules.
- Ensuring the changes made are updated in the CMDB/ CMS.
- Ensuring all change tasks are closed.
- Get involved in post implementation of the change and follow up for the successful migration of the release.
- Ensure all change requests are closed as per the defined SLA.

Change testing

Change testing is an activity of verifying and validating a changed CI (software program or hardware) ensuring that the CI meets the business and technical requirements, works as planned and expected, and can be implemented in the IT infrastructure.

So here are the steps to be done while performing the testing:

- Define the objective of testing
- Define a plan to test the change (who, what, when, where, etc.)
- Prepare or document the test cases
- Identify and understand the current configuration of the CI with respect to hardware configuration, software configuration, etc.
- Document the base lined information (If possible backup)
- Execute the test in a test environment (if a test environment is not available, then in a production environment) with respect to functionality, security, reliability, performance, usability
- Execute the regression and system testing
- Document the issues and observations
- Compare the data to your predictions

- Determine what modifications should be made
- Document the learning's and modifications that have to be made and submit it to the change manager or authorized role

Change impact analysis

Change impact analysis is an activity which discovers the negative effects or risks in a proposed change in the IT infrastructure. This activity helps you to identify the issues proactively and will aid you to define the remediation plans and corrective plans for any issues that may arise. Accordingly, the CAB determines to approve/reject the change request.

Change impact analysis can be assessed by checking the number of people (how many people will be affected), dependencies, consequences (vulnerabilities and threats), costs, and time required to implement a change, etc. It is assessed on various factors like structure (internal teams of IT), strategy (IT processes and policies), systems (hardware and software), stakeholders (customers, partners, suppliers, internal employees, etc) attitude, skills, and styles.

Approach for conducting impact analysis can be defined through the below mentioned steps:

- Assign a specific team (who has good experience in change management) for conducting impact analysis.
- Conduct a brainstorming session to identify:
    - Which customers will be impacted by the change?
    - Which partners will be impacted by the change?
    - Which suppliers will be impacted by the change?
    - How many stakeholders will be impacted?

  - What business processes will be impacted by the change?
  - What are the dependencies?
  - What IT services (storage service, communication service, etc) will be impacted by the change?
  - What software components (applications, databases, web servers, firewall, etc) will be impacted by the change?
  - What hardware components (storage space, processor, memory, etc) will be impacted by the change?
  - What IT processes and policies will be impacted?
- Assess if the brainstormed issues are valid
- Assess the consequences of the issues raised
- Develop mitigation plans

Change collisions and detection

Change collisions are the discrepancies that can arise when two or more changes are planned or scheduled for implementation (in the live environment) on the same CI at the same time.

When two changes are implemented at the same time on the same CI, it would result in some new incidents or will cost some extra or redundant work for the change implementation team. Hence, the change management team should check whether the planned changes conflict with other change requests with respect to affected CI or implementation time.

Hence, the change implementation team should do a meticulous check on the change requests and identify the change collisions, by capturing information like:

- Conflicting Change Request Numbers: RFCXXXX, RFCYYYY
- Conflict Type: Parent CI already scheduled, Child CI already scheduled, CI retired, etc.
- Affected CI
- CI relationship
- Duration
- Actual scheduled time
- Change implementer
- Location where the change will be implemented
- Risk associated
- Change collision identified by person
- Change collision identified by the tool

- Change collision identified date

And the detailed report is sent to the Change manager or to the defined role.

Automation in change management

Today, most of the organizations are having challenges in handling and implementing the changes successfully because of the inevitable complexity in IT systems, coordination with various teams involving different technologies, possible human errors, etc.

Hence, automation in change management is very essential to improve the percentage of successful changes, ensure change implementations bring positive results, detect unauthorized changes, reduce the time, efforts and risk of human errors. Automation in change management operations can be implemented in activities like:

- Usage of templates to create different RFCs (standard, normal, emergency, etc.)
- Impact estimation of a change
- Risk evaluation of a change
- Automatic transition of the change request from one phase to other after necessary approvals
- Automatic notifications, reminders, and emails to the stakeholders
- Identification of CI dependencies
- Prediction of change collisions

- Documentation of the changes
- Change reconciliation
- Change remediation
- Auditing the change request

Pre-requisites for automation in change management

- Accurate and detailed CI details in CMDB
- Defined process and workflow for different types of changes
- Stabilized CI architecture
- Thorough understanding on the functionality; the functionalities should be repeated
- Defined workflows for changing different attributes on a CI

Reports for change management

Some important reports that should be generated in change management are:

1. **Change Types** (which should give the numbers on emergency changes, normal changes, standard changes)

2. **Change Categories** (which should give information detailing where the change occurred like operating system, mainframes, applications, databases, servers, virtual machines)

3. **Change Phases** (which should give information detailing the different phases of change like registered, categorized, analysis, waiting for approval, approved, implementation, closed)

4. **Normal Changes by Date/Month** (which should give information about the normal changes with respect to dates)

5. **Emergency Changes by Date/Month** (which should give information about the emergency changes with respect to dates)

6. **Standard Changes by Date/Month** (which should give information about the standard changes with respect to dates)

7. **Average Time Taken to Implement a Change** (which should give information about the time taken to implement a change)

8. **Changes by Assignment** (which should give information about the people who handled the change)

All the above mentioned reports cannot be presented to all levels of management (top/high level, middle/tactical level, and low/operational level), reports sent to the audiences should give appropriate information which can help them to give a snapshot of the IT operations and should enable them to make effective decisions.

Hence top level management should get reports on:

- Number of changes with respect to type (standard change, normal change, and emergency change)
- Number of successful and failed changes
- Costs and time spent
- CSat on changes

Middle level management should get to see the reports on:

- Change categories (where the change occurred)
- Number of changes that created incidents

- Number of changes that were implemented in adherence to SLA
- Number of changes that breached SLA
- CRs/RFC which involved other process SMEs or third party companies

Low level management should get to see the reports on:

- Number of change requests logged with respect to date
- Number of change requests closed in a day
- Number of P1 changes
- Changes with respect to assignment
- Number of change requests with respect to phase (registered, analysis (Impact and Risk), waiting for approval, approved, implementation, PIR, closed)

Change Management for Consultants and Management

Implementing change management

Define

Prepare the project charter, consisting of a business case, SOW, MOSCOW analysis, goal statement, project plan, project scope, and roles and responsibilities.

Opportunity Statement – should define the issues in existing IT management/operations with respect to changes like:

- Failed changes due to lack of planning or unapproved changes
- Lack of knowledge materials or reference materials for planning and approving changes
- No standard process and procedures defined
- CAB approvals taking long time
- Escalations due to inappropriate changes

Business case - should describe the benefits and opportunities of change management considering the following areas:

- What are the short term benefits and long term benefits of this project?
- Does this new initiative align with other business processes if any exist?

- What impacts will this new initiative have on other business units and employees (pros and cons)?
- What are the most important services/CIs like VBFs or CBUs
- Number of increasing change requests in ITSM tool
- Should we have an explicit change management function or integrated change and release and deployment management?
- What are the risks and issues involved, and what are the dependencies?
- Estimations of costs on infrastructure assets (hardware, software, people-ware) and other miscellaneous things.

MOSCOW analysis - Should capture the requirements with respect to Must, Should, Could, and Would be (in future)

Statement of work (SOW) - Develop the SOW for the change management process, defining the:

- scope of services/products for which change management applies
- identification of service assets and CIs that are out of scope
- identification of critical services which has financial impact and impact on many users

- hardware, software and people required to manage change management as a process and operations

Goal statement – should be closely associated with the prepared business case and SOW. Goals should be SMART and mention:

- What are the CSFs?
- What are the KPIs?
- What is the time estimated to see the results?

Project interfaces - should define the boundaries, scope, relationships of the change management with other ITSM processes and functions.

Project plan - should show the timeline and milestones for various activities to establish change management process and run the operations.

Roles and responsibilities - should identify the required roles and hire human resources. The primary roles needed for change management can be defined as:

- Level 1 and Level 2 change analysts
- Change manager
- CAB (Change Advisory Board)

Also define RACI model for clarity in roles and responsibilities.

Measure

Measure phase should define the metrics and measurement plan for capturing the performance of change process and operations. These metrics should be defined based on customer requirements and acceptance criteria.

- Define measurement plan which addresses:
    - The historical information of change requests frequency, change types, changes from different services, and CIs
    - Who will do the measurement (Change Manager, Change Analysts, CAB, etc.)?
    - How will it be measured?
    - How often will it be measured (Daily, Weekly, Monthly)?
    - How will it be reported (PowerPoint presentation, Charts, Reports, etc.)
    - Define metrics for change management with respect to:
        - ✓ Criticality to Quality (Number of successful changes, Number of failed changes, Number of unapproved changes, Quality score that should be maintained, etc.)
        - ✓ Criticality to Process (Process adherence, etc.)
        - ✓ Criticality to Cost (Number of resources involved, Cost associated with a change, etc.)

  - ✓ Criticality to Delivery (Number of changes, number of emergency changes, etc.)
  - ✓ To know more details on metrics, check the section Metrics.

- Ensure those metrics are SMART (Specific, Measurable, Achievable, Relevant, and Time-bound)
- Define SLAs for change management - consulting SLM, and other ITSM processes (like Availability management, Capacity management, Information security management, Supplier management, etc.) as per the customer's requirements. The best practice on definition of SLAs:
  - ▪ For Greenfield project, define SLAs after understanding the operations for at least two months.
  - ▪ If there is any experienced staff person who worked as a change manager, you can take his/her experiences and baseline the SLAs, ensuring you could redefine them (if necessary) after checking two months of operations.
  - ▪ You can have a brainstorming session with all ITSM process owners and define SLAs; ensuring you could redefine them (if necessary) after checking two months of operations.

Analyze

The analyze phase should define high level process designs (linking customer requirements and acceptance criteria) identifying inputs, outputs, outcomes, triggers, interfaces, boundaries, exceptions, roles, etc.

- Understand the existing IT services to categorize and organize them into a hierarchy.
- Define the high level change management process with inputs, outputs, outcomes, triggers, interfaces, etc.
- Define the high level process depicting the change management roles and responsibilities.
- Define what databases would be needed for change management operations.
- Analyze what should be the criteria for major changes with respect to the number of people affected.
- Analyze what should be the criteria for standard changes, with respect to risk, cost, and scope of services.
- Analyze what should be the criteria for emergency changes, with respect to risk, cost, scope of services, SLAs.
- Analyze what should be the criteria for normal changes, with respect to risk, cost, and scope of services.
- Analyze what could be the potential risks when there are any changes on IT applications and CIs, IT storage services and CIs, IT network services and CIs, IT database services, etc.

Design

Design phase should define the detailed and complete process and procedures

- Define the hierarchy for organizing the changes

E.g.:

Hardware
desktop and accessories
laptop and accessories
servers and accessories
networking devices

Software
Operating system
Applications
Middleware
Databases

- Define procedures on how to handle a normal change.
- Define procedures on how to handle a standard change.
- Define procedures on how to handle an emergency change. For example:

- Registration and categorization → Accepted/Rejected → Assigned → Business case preparation → Risk and impact assessment → CAB approval/rejection → Coordination with release and deployment management

- Develop change models with respect to standard changes for different IT services.
- Define RFCs/change requests templates for services
- Define policies for RFCs/CRs:
  - identifying every RFC/CR with a unique number and naming convention
  - no change requests should be assigned to two or more change analysts
  - only authorized and approved changes should be implemented
  - all rejected changes should be notified to change requesters
  - all discussion points, action items, observations in CAB should be documented and sent to all change management, release and deployment, change evaluation, service validation and testing process owners and managers
- Define the impact and urgency levels as per the business requirements. For example:

Impact	Affected users
1	More than 1000 users
2	More than 500 users
3	More than 100 users
4	10-20 users

Urgency	To be implemented in
1	Less than 1 day
2	Less than 2-3 days
3	Less than 1 week
4	Less than 1 month

- Define appropriate ITSM or change management tool with respect to business requirements.
- Define what total details have to be encapsulated in change records.
  - basic details of RFC/CR (change requester name, change requester location, date and time when the CR was raised)
  - change registration number
  - description of the change
  - detailed description
  - business justification for change/business case
  - effect of not implementing change
  - affecting services
  - involved configuration items
  - impact
  - urgency

- risk assessments and analysis description
- CAB meetings discussions (date and time when the meetings happened, CAB members names, issues discussed, etc.)
- remediation and rollback plans details
- associated incidents tickets
- associated problem tickets
- associated change tickets
- lessons learned

- Define the change coordination procedures for normal, standard, and emergency changes.
- Define the criteria when a change request can be rejected.
- Define the templates for change back out, change remediation, test plan, etc.
- Define CAB members contacts list.
- Define IT contacts list responsible for different services (e.g. network, application server, etc.).
- Define training sessions on process, tools, technical knowledge, etc.
- Execute the change management operations.

Validate

Validate phase should define the V&V (verification and validation) and improvement activities to improve the process

- Ensure all the process collaterals are approved by the Service manager and agreed by other ITSM process owners like Release manager, Service validation and testing, Quality assurance manager, etc.
- Take feedback from all ITSM stakeholders on the definition new processes and procedures.
- Prioritize and act on the feedbacks and recommendations, if they make sense.
- Define procedures for staff and other ITSM stakeholders to give recommendations and feedback on the defined system.
- Ensure all CRs/RFCs are registered, categorized, tracked, and closed in the ITSM tool as per the defined procedures.
- Ensure the IT contacts list is regularly updated with all the necessary contact details.
- Ensure the change management operation is in consideration with metrics, and SLTs defined in SLAs.
- Perform RCA on all changes that failed, backed out, rolled out, and remediated.

Improving change management

Define

The define phase should define the improvement opportunities, business case, goal statement, project plan, and roles and responsibilities.

Opportunity Statement – should define the issues in existing change management operations such as:

- SLA breaches with respect change implementation
- No process definition or inefficient process definition
- No defined procedures for handling changes
- Failed changes or changes creating incidents
- Low scores in change ticket quality audits

Business case – should describe the benefits and opportunities of improving change management considering the following areas:

- What are the short term benefits and long term benefits of this project?
- What impacts will this new initiative have on other business units and employees (pros and cons)?
- Should we have an explicit change management or integrated change management and release and deployment management?
- Reason for initiating this improvement project should include:
    - Number of failed changes.
    - Number of change requests that aren't approved and are in pending status.
    - Costs involved in failed changes.

- Number of incidents that occurred due to failed changes.
- Dissatisfaction on the defined change process from the change management staff.
- Non conformances observed in internal audits or external audits.

Goal statement – should be focusing on business goals and IT goals

- Should define what is the improvement, and what the team is aiming to accomplish?
- What is the estimated time for delivery of results?
- What are the tangible result deliverables?

Project plan – should show the milestones and time estimation for the activities involved in improving change management as a process and operations.

Roles and responsibilities – should identify the required roles. Primary roles needed for change management can be defined as:

- change manager
- change advisory board members (which includes ECAB, DCAB, TCAB, etc.)
- change analysts

Define RACI model for clarity in roles and responsibilities.

Measure

The measure phase should capture as much as information about the current operations to understand how it is being operated and how well it is being operated. It also includes setting up the baselines as the basis for the improvement.

- Understand the IT services running in the organization.
- Understand the scope of services for change management, and if there is any scope creep in any instances.
- Determine if the current scope is good enough for change management operations.
- Understand who are the teams, raising maximum number of change requests (standard, normal, and emergency changes).
- Understand where there are maximum numbers of changes (standard, normal, and emergency changes).
- Identify the trends of changes where there is maximum number of changes with respect to services.
- Identify the criteria, rules, and specifications for creating RFCs
- Identify who are the stakeholders who have privileges to create RFCs
- Understand the existing process
- Understand how the BIA is estimated
- Understand what are the risk mitigation procedures and how risks are identified
- Understand what is the criteria for major and minor changes
- Identify all the changes that have failed, backed out, rolled back and categorize them into groups (changes

with respect to databases, changes with respect to networks, changes related to application servers, etc.)

- Identify all the changes that have created incidents (major incidents, minor incidents)
- Check with change management staff on whether or not they have clarity and understanding on the processes and procedures.
- Talk with change management staff personnel's to check what was good/bad/what was missing in the existing process and procedures.
- Identify the changes that breached the SLAs.
- Perform baselines of the current change management operations.

Analyze

Analyze phase should identify the gaps and root causes for the discrepancies in CM process and operations. It also includes analyzing if the process collaterals were well defined like processes, RACI matrix, SOPs, CSFs, KPIs, metrics, and etc.

- Analyze what are the gaps in existing CM process and also procedures for operational teams, with respect to ISO/IEC20K standard.
- Analyze if the CSFs, KPIs, and metrics are aligned towards the IT goals.
- Analyze the existing metrics and SLAs, if they are feasible.

- Analyze if the BIA is performed correctly; identify the discrepancies if there are any.
- Analyze the risk mitigation methods and procedures and identify the gaps.
- Analyze if there any discrepancies in the criteria with respect to major and minor changes.
- Identify the root causes for all the failed changes (if they are less in number) or a sample of failed changes.
- Identify the root causes for all the changes that breached SLAs or a sample of breached SLAs.
- Check if the staff is able to meet the defined metrics and SLAs.
- Identify the root causes for all the changes or a sample of changes that have been in "Waiting for approval" status.
    - Check if there were enough reference materials available in the knowledge base, and if the knowledge in reference materials was technically accurate.
    - Were there any contact details discrepancies?
    - Was the CM staff unaware of the process and procedures?
- Analyze the reasons why emergency changes were failing.
- Analyze the reasons why normal changes were failing.

- Identify the flaws or misses in the existing process with respect to the business scenario by checking:
    - if the process is aligned to business objectives
    - if the process provides clarity in roles and responsibilities
    - if the process is complete, and there is enough guidance for all the scenarios that can happen in the change lifecycle
    - If the process is clearly written without any ambiguity
    - If the process is aligned to the best practices and standards
    - If the process is repeatable

Note: Analysis on all the above activities can be done by brainstorming with the key stakeholders of change management team, ITSMO (IT Service management officer), ITSM manager and IT manager.

Improve

Improve phase aims at improving the current process and operations, with creative solutions to eliminate the root causes in order to fix and prevent process and operational discrepancies.

- Involve all the key stakeholder from CM and other ITSM process and brainstorm how to improve the CM process and operations.

- List all the discussed ideas, and propose your ideas:
  - Redefining the CSFs, KPIs and metrics consulting SLM, as per the customer's requirements. Metrics should be defined in alignment to:
    - ✓ Customer's priorities, requirements, and acceptance criteria
    - ✓ Most important services
  - Redefine the change management process ensuring:
    - ✓ There is a clear definition, demarcation and conditions on normal, standard and emergency change
    - ✓ There is a clear definition on impact, urgency, and prioritization
    - ✓ There is a clear definition of inputs, triggers, outputs and interfaces for the process.
    - ✓ There is a clear definition of change models for different services
    - ✓ There is a change coordinators contacts list.
    - ✓ There are defined procedures for assessing the business risk and technical risks
    - ✓ There is a defined test plan focusing on functionality, usability, performance, security, availability, etc. for every change request.
    - ✓ There is a defined procedure for the change manager with respect to daily job activities
    - ✓ There are workflows/flowcharts that are easily understandable
- Seek approvals from the Service Manager & Process owner on the redefined process collaterals.

- Ensure that all staff is aware on the usage of the change management tool with respect to change planning, collisions, impact analysis, etc.
- Define policies to conduct training sessions on process, knowledge, tool knowledge, etc.
- Define policies to assess the staff knowledge, conducting exams, quizzes, etc.
- Provide access to CMDB for all change management staff

Control

Control phase defines the V&V (verification and validation) and continuous improvement activities that should be performed on change process and operations.

- Monitor the change management operations for the next two months, ensuring that all staff follows the defined processes and procedures.
- Check if the operational staff involved in change management is good to manage the number of changes requests occurring.
- Ensure that the change management staff is aware of the SLAs for all services.
- Check if the staff is able to meet the defined metrics and SLAs.
- Ensure all change requests are being tracked in the defined tool.
- Check the change requests which have breached the SLAs and perform the root cause analysis.
- Document the lessons learned.

- Update the process again if there are any changes in the business requirements.
- Prepare monthly reports (including accomplishments, targets met as per SLA, targets breached, total number of changes logged and implemented, successful changes, failed changes, failed changes that created incidents; they should include financial information about the changes and incidents that are unresolved).
- Collect feedback from operational staff and customers.

Change Management in Devops approach

Devops is a word framed by combining two words: development and operations. It is an approach to get development teams and operational teams work closely together to eliminate gaps like code stabilization issues, inappropriate capacity and availability designs, inappropriate test environment, inappropriate deployment instructions, application instability, tools incompatibility with other applications/tools, no proper handover, etc.

The goal of devops approach is to have seamless communication to all the stakeholders involved in the service development, increase the speed and decrease the friction in deployment of services (faster delivery of application development or enhancements).

By following devops approach, change management can provide great value to ITSM processes and IT operations and they would work as described below:

Following devops approach, service strategy processes (like strategy generation, demand management, service portfolio management, business relationship management) would communicate the upcoming changes/new services to the change management process owner. This will aid the service strategy stakeholders to get to know if the change can really provide some VOI/ ROI, what are the associated risks, vulnerabilities, and issues in-advance by change management staff. Accordingly, the service strategy manager and stakeholders will take the preventive actions on new/changed services in the initiation stage itself.

Also the change management team will be able to understand the strategy, demands, business and customer requirements, type of users, etc. right from the beginning and will have a complete idea about the change.

Following devops approach, service design processes (like availability management, capacity management, information security management, supplier management, service level management, IT service continuity management) would communicate and collaborate with change management process owner and this would enable the change manager to understand the service level requirements, service level agreements, high level architecture, metrics, capacity and availability designs, security designs, etc. with respect to new services or changed services.

This will help the change management staff to plan and test the changes thoroughly and also it will help the service design stakeholders to get to know the risks, vulnerabilities, and issues in-advance through the change management staff. Accordingly, the service design manager and stakeholders will take the preventive actions on new/changed services in the design stage itself.

Following devops approach, service transition processes (like release and deployment, service validation and testing, change evaluation, knowledge management, configuration management) would benefit to a great extent as change management is involved in the new/changed service development right from the strategy stage it would be having perfect idea on any new/changed services and accordingly they will able to define perfect transition plans, collaterals for all service transition activities like approvals on changes, knowledge articles creation, FSC, PSO, etc.

Following devops approach, service operations processes (like service request fulfilment, incident, problem, access, event management) would communicate and collaborate with change management process owner and change manager, giving information on the potential risks with respect to new changes. Also service operational processes (like incident, problem, access, event management) would be able to get up to date information about the changes and releases happening in the infrastructure, which enables them to understand the incidents happening.

Note: CSI would anyways interact with all processes and functions in the IT service lifecycle.

Change Management with SCRUM approach

Scrum is a framework which uses iterative and incremental practices based on the agile project management methodology aiming at increased productivity, quality of deliverables, and reduced efforts and time duration.

ITSM change management can also be executed by following SCRUM approach as described below:

Change manager as Product owner

The Product Owner can be considered as a Change Manager who will be accountable for ensuring that the team delivers value to business.

- He allocates the skilled team members to work on a specific change ticket.
- He defines the customer centric items or change tickets (user stories) and adds them to the product backlog to act immediately.
- Ensures the process is followed as defined
- Organize meetings with all CAB members, technical SMEs, and other ITSM stakeholders
- Accept or reject the RFCs

Prioritized list of change tickets as Product backlog

Prioritized list of change tickets can be considered as product backlog which is an ordered and prioritized list of change tickets as per the SLAs, risk associated, dependencies, etc.

- Product backlog will be managed and owned by change manager
- It can be changed and re-prioritized before selection of each change ticket

Change investigation and assessment activities as Sprint backlog

Change investigation and assessment activities like impact analysis, change tasks creation, change tasks scheduling and planning can be considered as sprint backlog.

- Each activity's status should be tracked, and a specific person would be responsible to carry out the activity.
- Each activity's status is updated on daily basis.

Burndown chart for every change ticket

A burndown chart for every change should depict the total man days proposed and number of man days spent; it should ideally burn down to zero to the end of the sprint.

Sprint reviews for every change ticket

Sprint reviews should be conducted for every change ticket to check if the change ticket has been well documented, tasks are created, all approvals have been made, and all risks and its associated mitigation plans are documented.

- Participants in the sprint review should be the internal change management team staff.

Sprint retrospective

Sprint retrospective would be the last thing done in a sprint. As always, there is an opportunity to improve; hence, this retrospective is performed after approving and implementing the change.

- Participants in the sprint review should be – change manager, problem manager, CSI manager, availability manager, information security manager, capacity manager, etc.
- To identify the lessons learned, to identify the mistakes that were done while handling the changes, and to identify more efficient ways for conducting analysis.

Integrating Change and Release management

ITSM processes can be integrated with other ITSM processes which will enable it in reducing the costs on human resources (having multiple roles as process owners) and also reduces complexities.

Here is a list of scenarios where change management can be integrated with other processes and functions:

Integrated Change Management with Change Evaluation, Release and deployment and Service Validation and Testing

Integration of CM, CE, RDM and SVT is possible, provided there is demarcation of roles and responsibilities and SOPs for the staff in the integrated process. This can be done by assigning:

Change level 1 analysts to analyze the registered RFCs/change requests, assess the impact and identify the dependencies on services and assets, categorize them, prioritize them, and define the change plans detailing the EU benefits, IT benefits, and business benefits. They would also be in charge of grouping and relating changes.

Change level 2 analysts/evaluators would shadow the work done by level 1 analysts, and add those extra details and information as necessary to make the change plans more detailed, accurate and complete. Also they evaluate the change plans made for the respective RFCs.

CAB would do the analysis of the change and release plans and would decide whether the change and release has to be approved or rejected.

Change implementers / Release and deployment analysts will develop the build and deployment plans, ELS (Early Life Support) training materials and release approach strategies.

Service validation and test analysts would do the evaluation of individual releases, end to end service after a release is deployed, documentation with respect to release, etc.

Due diligence questions for change management

Due diligence in IT operations is an activity which conducts an investigation into operations; it ensures that you have access to all important information about the IT operations that you are going to manage. It enables you to assess the contracts, intellectual property, current operations, risks, issues, legal and regulatory compliance associated.

Due diligence questions for change management can be mentioned as:

- What are the customer pain points with respect to change management?
- What is the scope of services for change management operations (like applications, infrastructure, etc.)?
- Are there any internal/external suppliers involved in supporting the change management operations?
- Is there a defined SLA for change management operations?
- What are SLTs defined for normal/standard/emergency/any other changes?
- What is the average change resolution time for a normal, standard, and emergency change?
- What all regions do you support with respect to change management operations?
- Who are your major customers?

- Do you have defined change management process and policies?
- What are the KPIs and metrics defined for change management operations?
- Does your change management staff follow the process and policies? Or is there any resistance?
- What is the current staff allocated for change management (like change manager, change initiator, implementers, CAB)?
- Is there a defined organizational chart and roles and responsibilities defined?
- What are the different tools used for change management?
- Is the team well trained on tools?
- Do you have access to any other tools like monitoring, incident management, problem management, release and deployment, knowledge management, configuration management, etc.?
- What are the CIs (databases/applications/mainframes/etc.) which trigger maximum number of changes?
- Are all the changes registered, categorized, prioritized, assessed, and approved?
- Is there any method for performing cost benefit analysis on changes requested?

- What are the different types of changes handled in current operations like standard, normal, emergency, expedite, unplanned, etc.?
- Who has the privileges to raise change requests?
- What is the total number of change requests raised in a month?
- What is the number of normal change/standard change/emergency change requests received in a month?
- What is the % of successful changes in a month?
- What is the % of failed changes in a month?
- Is there any defined methodology for doing the risk and impact analysis for change requests?
- Is there a defined methodology for testing the changes?
- Do you have any database defined for archiving all change requests?
- Is there a defined knowledge base and defined change management operations; what is the number of knowledge articles defined for changes?
- Is the change management tool integrated to any CMDB/CMS tools?
- Would the customer staff involve in CAB members list?
- In a week, how many CAB meetings happen?
- In a week, how many E-CAB meetings happen?

- What are the different kinds of reports generated and shared with customer?
- What is the reason for outsourcing change operations?
- Have you ever outsourced the operations before? What were the issues you had with your previous supplier?

Change management in IT technologies

Change management in clouds

Change management is the most nitty-gritty process for cloud environment as cloud is based on distributed computing, shared services, and converged infrastructure; any unplanned/negligent changes and untested changes would lead to major incidents impacting huge number of incidents.

In a cloud environment, it is very common that a CSP (Cloud Service Provider) will have to do hundreds of changes in a year. Be it any service models like IaaS, PaaS, SaaS, etc. CSP will have to do numerous changes with respect to hardware configuration, software, and documentation; hence, CSP definitely needs the change management process to avoid any kind of discrepancies while implementing the changes.

Change management in cloud

As cloud is based on pay per use model, users can change their requirements as per the need and these change requests in clouds can be triggered for various reasons as mentioned below:

- a service request is created by an end user or customer seeking for a change (add/ modify/ delete) his existing service.

  Example: An end user currently uses Microsoft office cloud services like MS-Word, Powerpoint, Excel and now needs to use Visio for 1 month; so he/she would place a service request to have Visio access enabled for his/her login credentials.

Or End user asking for more storage space in his virtual desktop.

- a new business requirement from the customer or from any other stakeholders like legal, etc.

  Example: As per country's new legal requirement all CSP's should follow the ISO/IEC20K standard for managing the IT services

- an error or failure that has occurred in a specific software/hardware with respect to cloud service.

Change types in cloud environment

Change types in a cloud environment can be classified into three types as request for change for new requirements (RFC-FNR), request for change for resolving incidents (RFC-FRI), and request for change for routine operations (RFC-FRO).

Examples on RFC-FNR: As per country's new legal requirement all CSP's should follow the ISO/IEC20K standard for managing the IT services

Examples on RFC-FRI: An error or failure that has occurred in a specific software/ hardware with respect to cloud service.

Examples on RFC-FRO: An end user requests for more storage space on his virtual desktop

And further these change types can be classified into three categories as standard, normal and emergency changes as mentioned in ITSM best practices.

Processing of a change request in cloud

- An end user places a request for some addition or modification or deletion of services.
- The Change Management team will verify and validate the EU's request and his details through a callback and will process the change request for registration.
- The Change Management team will segregate the change request as RFC-FNR, RFC-FRI and RFC-FRO; and will categorize the change type as normal, standard, and emergency.
- The Change Management team will analyze the impact, urgency, target CI/Service, etc.
- If it's a RFC-FNR/RFC-FRO, the Change Management team will forward the RFC information to financial team for changing the billing or payment terms based on the RFC.
- Change management team will follow the respective model (standard/normal/emergency) based on the CSP's policies and EU's request; accordingly RFCs will be assigned to release and deployment team for scheduling and implementation.

Best practices for cloud customers with respect to changes

Cloud service providers do continuous improvements on their services through numerous updates, so if the customers accept all changes/releases into the operational environment without assessing the risks associated it would lead to many incidents. Hence, here are some best practices that has to be followed by the customers who are using cloud services especially in PaaS & IaaS.

- Know the FSCs

  Customers should get the information on the FSCs giving information on the details the changes, scheduled date, maintenance window time, etc.

- Try the POC

  Before planning and implementing a new release in the environment, the team should experience the POC (Proof Of Concept) to understand the new features and how they fit in with your environment. Customers should have a sandbox to try out the new releases.

- Test the releases

  Customers should ensure appropriate testing is performed on every release to ensure it works in the operational environment considering their operational environment (applications and databases), number of users (load and stress testing), other integrated systems, etc.

- Perform risk analysis on every new release

  Customers should definitely perform risk analysis before implementing a new release into the operational environment; and they should inform the risks identified to the CSP to check if there are any mitigating procedures.

- Information on known errors

  Customers should get to know the known errors, its associated temp fix and perm fix with respect to every release.

- Implementation in phased approach

  Customers should not implement any updates/up-gradations straight to the operational environment in a big-bang approach; it is always advisable to do such updates in an incremental and phased approach.

Change management in software environment

Changes in software would obviously lead to changes in IT systems, and changes in IT systems would lead to changes in business processes.

Hence, ITSM best practices define a common process and process activities for change management which can be implemented in software/hardware environment. But again, the processes defined by popular ITSM best practices are at 30K feet high which doesn't give the precise details how changes are managed in software environment.

Hence, this topic would give you the insight concerning software changes and change management in the software environment. Software changes are those changes that have to be implemented in a software environment with respect to new requirements in software, errors, performance, security, availability, etc.

Software change requests can be classified into four types as described below:

- Bug fix
- Enhancement
- Architecture maintenance
- Software reengineering

Bug fix requests are those repairs made to a program or software to correct deficiencies or defects or errors so that the software meets its defined requirements.

Enhancement requests are those new proposals that improve the software with respect to functionality (adding or changing features).

Architecture maintenance requests are those which actually change the architecture of the software, which enables the software to work in a different operating environment (hardware or software), and which improves or upgrades the non-functional requirements like performance, security, availability, etc.

Software engineering requests are those which actually restructure and reorganize the software to facilitate future changes.

Process flow for change management in software environment

RFC registration → Requirements analysis → Requirements consolidation → Impact analysis (Analyze source code) → Risk analysis → Modify source code → Change testing → Change approval → Change Implementation (build/test/production environments)

RFC Registration: This is the phase where the change requests will be registered with a unique id, basic details, associated CI, description, etc. Change requests in form of bug fixes, enhancements, architecture maintenance requests, engineering requests are received here.

Requirements Analysis: This is the phase where the change requests will be analyzed thoroughly to understand what are the business requirements, technical requirements, user requirements, etc.

Requirements Consolidation: This is the phase where the gathered requirements are consolidated in a tool and confirmed with the respective stakeholders.

Impact Analysis: This is the phase where the change will be analyzed and the analysis is done on the source code, to understand the possible implications of making change. It identifies all the files, models, and documents that have to be modified for incorporating the requested change.

Risk Analysis: This is the phase where the risks will be identified, analyzed, and assessed; accordingly mitigation plans are defined.

Modify Source Code: This is the phase where the change is implemented by doing the modifications to the source code.

Change Testing: This is the phase where the verification and validation happens in the development and test environment.

Change Approval: This is the phase where the change approval happens and where this approval will be done by a group of SMEs considering different functional and technical aspects.

Change Implementation: This is the phase where the changes are grouped together and accordingly where release and deployment work will be carried out.

Issues without software change management

Lack of software change management process and process adherence would lead to severe issues such as:

- Poor software quality
- Rework
- Failed changes
- Downtime in production
- Longer processing time for implementing changes

Advice and Interview Questions for Change Management Roles

Interview Questions for Change management

How can I define a categorization structure for change tickets?

Change categorization can be done in three types as:

- Normal changes
- Standard changes
- Emergency changes

All the three change categories of change tickets can be structured using CTS (Category and Subcategory) classification; hence, I would be discussing more in detail how you can segregate change tickets as mentioned below:

Category: Hardware changes (with respect to IT), Software changes (with respect to IT), Facilities changes

Subcategory: Computer, Network, Storage, Voice, Application, Database, etc.

More detailed view on change category

Hardware changes can be classified as
Servers
Client systems

Mainframe
Laptop
Desktop
PDAs
Printing and scan devices
Networking devices
Power systems
Temperature maintenance systems

Software changes can be classified as
Operating system
Virtual operating system
Virtual computer
Web software
Database
Applications

You may also include another classification as "cause" representing availability issues, security issues, performance issues, etc.

What are the pros of standard changes?

The pros of standard changes can be described as:

- Low in risk
- Rapid implementation of changes in less time duration and with better planning
- Defined change window
- No unauthorized changes

What is the criterion to say that a change involves complexity?

Change can be said characterized as complex when:

- The change is difficult to be backed out
- There are too many risks associated with a change
- There are many teams being involved in implementing the change
- The change has impact on multiple business processes
- The estimated downtime for a change is too long

What is the criterion to say that a change request is a major change?

Criteria for a major change can be described as the:

- Changes that have impact on multiple business processes

- Change that has impact on multiple users
- Changes that have impact on critical applications which should have high availability %

What are the examples of normal, standard, and emergency changes?

Normal change – Upgrading memory on a server machine.

Standard change – Patch installations on a specific day in a week.

Emergency change – Critical server hung, and it needs a restart.

How to prioritize changes?

Prioritizing changes can be done by defining impact and urgency which will be done based on the SLAs signed with customers. Here is my opinion on how you can define impact, urgency, and priority codes:

Impact	**Affected users**
1	More than 100 users
2	More than 50 users
3	More than 10 users
4	1-2 users

Urgency	Should be implemented in
1	Less than 1 day
2	Less than 1 week
3	Less than 15 days
4	Less than 1 month

Priority	Code
1	Critical
2	High
3	Average
4	Low

Common issues in change management which creates discrepancies?

- Mismatch between categorization of change tickets in change management tools and release and deployment tools.
- Mismatch between prioritization calculations in change management tools and release and deployment tools.
- Lack of communication or proper interlock meetings between change management staff and release management staff.
- Inappropriately defined or lack of RACI matrix.

- Unclear understanding on standard, normal, and emergency change.
- Improper risk and impact assessments.
- Usage of ambiguous classification in CTI like 'miscellaneous', 'others', 'unknown', etc.
- Both change management and release management managed by the same team, leading to inappropriate testing.
- Different individual tools being used for different ITSM processes.

How to identify the risk levels in change requests?

As we all know risk can be represented as risk = severity * likelihood.

A CR/RFC can be said to have high risk when:

- the change is implemented in business hours
- when there is no back-out, remediation, and rollback plans
- when there was no testing done

Are there any defined criteria for rejecting changes?

Change requests can be rejected when the change requests do not follow the process, policies, and procedures.

To make it more precise in operational language, a change can be rejected when:

- the change request is incomplete
- there is no back-out, remediation, and rollback plans
- there is no testing performed
- the approvals are not done
- the change requests are wrongly categorized or prioritized

What are the personal skills needed by a change manager?

- Assertive nature
- Analytical skills
- Good planning skills

What is the difference between change back out and change rollback?

Change back out is an activity where the change is half way executed (but not implemented completely) and realized that the change wouldn't be successful. So the rollback plan is executed to restore the earlier baseline of a service/CI.

Change rollback is an instance where the change implementation is completed, but testing does not yield expected results; hence, the decision is made to restore the services/CIs to earlier baseline status.

What is the difference between the rollback plan and remediation plan?

The remediation plan is a plan that details the alternative steps which has to be followed to minimize the risk, when a planned change does not deliver expected results.

The rollback plan is a plan that details how to restore the service/CI when a change fails completely or doesn't meet the acceptance criteria.

How would you ensure that the change management process is followed thoroughly by your team?

- By giving training sessions on the change management process, explaining the benefits of the process, policies and procedures and how it would reduce their overwork or discrepancies that have occurred in the past.
- By giving trainings on usage of the tool with respect to RFC statuses flow (RFC creation, approval, change tasks creation, etc.)

How can you ensure that the CMDB is updated after every change/release implementation?

Every change request should be classified into change tasks with respect to functionality of the work (like planning, build, testing, deployment, etc.).

So you should be creating a change task for the configuration manager to do the necessary updates with respect to the changes made in the CI.

So it becomes the responsibility of configuration manager to update the CMDB as per the change tasks assigned; and accountability lies with change manager to ensure that the CMDB is up-to-date.

What is a failed change?

A failed change is a change that was not implemented successfully or which did not produce the expected results as planned.

What would be the possible reasons for failures of changes?

Some of the possible reasons for failures of changes are:

- Inappropriate testing
- Improper communication
- Lack of rollback plans
- Improper risk and impact assessment

What happens when a change gets failed?

Generally, a change ticket has **n** number of change tasks; if any major tasks have failed then the change is considered to be failed.

Once the change ticket is considered as failed then immediately PIR has to be conducted to understand the reasons for failure. And accordingly another change request is raised.

If a change request is targeting modifications in three different CIs associated with a single service, would you create 3 CRs/RFCs?

The general practice is we create one change request and create three change tasks, and then assign these tasks to the respective technical teams to do the necessary changes.

So there would be only one change request.

How can I come to know that a change has been implemented on a CI/Service when there is no change record?

It is a tedious task to identify the successful changes that has been implemented but yet it's definitely possible by analyzing the CMDB baselines and snapshots.

Identifying a failed change is easy because when you perform the analysis of the incident/problem, then you get to know that it was because of a change. When you don't find a CR/RFC in the ITSM tool, it's clear.

When do I have to create a change record?

The change record should be created for all changes requests which are categorized as emergency/normal/major changes. The objective of creating a change record is that it encapsulates all the information of change and will be useful for future references.

How to assess the impact of a change?

The impact of a change can be assessed by:

- Understanding the CMDB to understand the associated services.
- Checking the SLAs to understand the criticality of the service.
- Getting in touch with the local IT staff (of that specific area where the incident occurred) to understand the impact of the incident.

Can RCA happen on change tickets and implemented changes?

Yes, RCA can happen on any unknown underlying issue which causes any incidents or reduction in the quality of service or failure of a service.

So RCA can also be conducted on failed changes, remediated changes, backed out changes and changes that are rolled back.

My change management operations manage numerous customers, can I manage all of the changes (from different customers) in one single tool?

No, it cannot be done; it would be better to have different teams and tools with respect to supporting customer. As the SLAs and metrics for every customer would be different.

I want to set up change management process in my organization. Is there any prerequisite process or function that is must for change management?

It would good to have configuration management process as a prerequisite for defining change management.

Who should be involved in PIR?

Primary stakeholders should be change implementer, change manager, CAB, release manager, test analysts, build and deployment analysts, and CSI manager.

What should the PIR contain?

PIR should capture all the important information on a change request, detailing:

- Change number
- Change description
- Change category
- Stakeholders involved (Change analyst, implementer, CAB staff, Change manager)
- Scheduled change implementation date and time

- Actual change implementation date and time
- List of CIs & Business Services that were impacted on account of the change
- Test results
- RCA if the change failed
- What was done well and what are the things where we could have done better
- Additional review comments/feedbacks
- Lessons learned

Should the PIR happen for only failed changes?

No, PIR should happen for all normal, emergency, failed, and backed out changes.

Can a single release have multiple changes?

Yes, it can have multiple changes. ITIL defines a release as a change or a collection of changes that are planned, built, tested, and deployed in a live IT environment.

Can a single release have different types of changes (normal, standard, and emergency)?

First of all, we should understand that different changes (normal, standard, and emergency) will have its own procedures to plan, categorize, assess, and approve them.

So consolidating all these normal, standard and emergency changes would become complicated.

At the same time, I wouldn't say that it's impossible; as it depends on the scenario. If these different types of changes are associated to a same CI/service, then yes all types of changes can be consolidated into a release and it can be deployed.

What aspects should be considered while doing risk assessments on RFCs/changes?

Risk assessments should focus on the four aspects as described below:

- Business risks (with respect to continuity).
- IT service risks (with respect to IT service continuity).
- Technical risks (with respect to CIs stability/reliability).
- People related risks (with respect to adherence and acceptance).

And these risks can be categorized into 3 levels as: High - 1, Medium - 2, Low - 3.

What is the difference between Risk analysis and Impact analysis in change management?

Risk analysis is the activity which checks the risks (unavailability of a service, slow performance, etc.) associated in implementing a change.

And impact analysis is the activity which checks the number of people and departments who will be impacted by the change.

If getting the change approvals from different stakeholders on a RFC is taking long time, how can we reduce the time duration (on change approvals)?

Reduce the number of approvers! Make a single person as accountable who should approve/reject the change. If he has to get inputs from various other stakeholders, he can brainstorm with the stakeholders at a certain point of time and approve the change or reject it. So, this would avoid wastage of time on chasing different stakeholders to get the approvals done.

How to control unauthorized changes?

Unauthorized changes can be controlled by:

- Conducting audits on all changes before implemented, to see there is CABs approval, back out plan, remediation plan
- Appropriate education and awareness about the process and procedures

How do I run the show (and it's business critical to implement the change) if my change management tool is down?

Any tool in ITSM would be useful for tracking, automating, reporting and analysis work at quicker time; so even if the tool is down, your changes can be registered, categorized, prioritized, scheduled, tested, approved, and implemented manually by documenting them on papers, inviting the CAB members to a meeting, taking the approvals and implementing them in operational environment.

What are the important artifacts needed for implementing standard changes?

Important artifacts needed for executing/implementing standard changes are:

- Defined standard change models for different kinds of services
- Requesting model/workflow or a tool through which requesters can raise standard change requests
- Standard change approver
- CAB (optional)

How to reduce emergency changes?

Emergency changes are the changes which actually create maximum chaos in IT environment; this can be reduced by:

- Setting predefined targets for change managers that they can have only 1%-2% of E-RFCS in a month
- Clearly educating the importance of E-RFC
- Clearly setting the criteria when an E-RFC can be raised.

- Having monthly calls with all change managers to identify who has approved the maximum number of ERFCs in a month like a NAME AND SHAME call.

Is it okay to send a RFC for CAB approval that is a month ahead to the implementation date?

Yes, it is okay; that gives the change analysts time to thoroughly plan the RFCs and also if they have to rework any aspect (if the CAB has rejected it once and provided some feedback, then they can work and resubmit it) it would be helpful.

When should the release management team be informed about the upcoming changes?

The release manager or release management team should be informed or involved right at the stage of CAB meetings, so that they have thorough understanding on the RFC.

As a CAB member, how do you ensure that change has been tested?

Every RFC, before being sent to CAB, has to be updated. With test plan made and test results accordingly, CAB would be able to approve the change.

Is it okay to implement the emergency change first and then do the recording and approving in tool?

Absolutely, No. Emergency changes have to recorded, analyzed, approved, tested and then only afterwards has to be implemented.

What are the different roles that you know in change management process?

Roles can be defined as per the organizational policies which are based on budget, scope of the services, and human resources. The common roles defined in change management operations are: Change initiator, Change manager, CAB, Change implementer, and Change verifier.

Why do you think categorization of changes is good?

Categorization of changes is good because:

- It defines specific process for a different kind of change which will help in speeding up the approval process.
- It will help to identify the number of standard/emergency/normal changes.
- It will help to balance the risk with defined procedures like ECAB/ TCAB/ DCAB meetings.
- It will help the team to drive priority, risk, lead times.

Who decides the downtime for a RFC?

Downtime is calculated by consulting the CI owners, Availability manager, and Service owner.

What is a change freeze period? Why should you have it?

Change freeze is a control mechanism for reducing the number of change requests. It is a point in time when the change management team decides to work on another business critical activity.

Change freeze period is rolled out when an organization is:

- at the financial year end
- at the holiday season
- deployment/migration of a new product

How would you determine the quality of an implemented change?

A quality change is one that is successful and which:

- is implemented as per the timelines and human resources allocated
- meets business needs and expectations
- does not create any incidents or problems
- doesn't have known errors

What would be the primary causes of failed changes in your experience?

Primary causes could be defined as:

- Insufficient testing
- No back-out plan and rollback plans defined
- Change collisions
- Variance in test and production environment

Should all P1 changes be treated as Major changes?

No, P1 changes cannot be called as major changes.

P1 actually signifies the priority of a change which is determined by the priority calculators or assessments done on impact and urgency.

And major changes are those changes which has impact on business critical services and impacts huge number of users.

Who should decide if a change is a major change or not?

Major changes criteria should be clearly defined by the customers like:

- if a change can impact more than 20 IT applications of an organization
- if there is a change which can impact on XX number of users

- If a change can create a risk of XX$ to the organization

Ideally, the Change Manager would be the accountable person; and he/she can consult with CAB members to decide if a change is a major change.

When and how are emergency changes triggered?

Emergency changes are those changes that have to be implemented through emergency procedures to correct any issue/issues on business critical systems.

It doesn't mean it's only meant for resolving major incidents; it could also be implemented to avoid major incidents and for business critical requirements from customer/ legal/ etc.

What is the difference between standard change and service request?

Standard changes are those changes (addition/modification deletion to existing IT services) that have been observed and implemented before; hence, they have predefined steps to follow. But yes, there is still a quotient of risk associated in standard changes; hence, it still requires change manager's and CABs approval to get implemented.

Service requests are those requests generated by the users through service catalog like request for information, request for a new device, request for approvals. Here there is no risk associated.

Can you have daily CAB meeting?

Yes, it depends on the number of change requests in the backlog.

What are the main skills needed for a change manager?

Main skills needed for change manager would be:

- Thorough knowledge on ITIL Service transition processes
- Understanding on ITIL all lifecycle modules
- Knowledge on risk management
- Negotiation skills
- Communication skills
- Assertive nature

Do we still need a rollback plan even if the change has no impact on users?

Yes, we would still need a rollback plan. And there would be no change request which has no impact on a user.

How do you ensure that the CMDB is updated after change implementation?

After every change implementation, the change manager has to update the details of the RFC to the configuration manager and CMDB administrator. Accordingly, once the updating is done, the change manager has to be informed about it.

What are the common issues which delay change requests implementation?

Common issues that delay the change requests implementation are:

- Change requests assigned to wrong assignment groups
- Change requests assigned to wrong approvers
- Slow approvals
- Inappropriate back-out & test plans

What is the difference between RFC and software code change?

RFC is a request where a stakeholder raises a request for change in IT environment (be it hardware/ software), and it will be addressed by IT change management process and its team.

Software code change is a ground level activity performed by the software developers following the defined change procedures or policies.

What is change backlog?

The change backlog is the number of change requests in the change management team member's queue which are not yet handled/processed/implemented.

For example: RFCs that have not been approved by the CAB or Change Manager.

What would be your approach for reducing the number of emergency changes?

Approach for reducing the number of emergency changes would be:

- Gather information on the historical emergency changes
- Identify the trends of E-changes which CIs generated maximum E-changes
- Perform the RCA why E-changes were raised
- Get in touch with respective stakeholders (process owner, service owner and SMEs) and update the issues observed to take corrective and preventive actions

Should I have different change management processes defined for different areas like data center/network/application environment?

No, organization should have only one process. Operating procedures for assessing, evaluating, testing, implementing, etc. can be different but the process should be only one.

Can we create a problem record for emergency change requests?

Emergency change requests are normally created when there is an emergency business requirement or when there is a major incident or when there is critical incident.

So, if there is an emergency change created for major incidents or critical incidents, yes you can create a problem ticket to understand why we created the emergency change.

If there are too many emergency changes on a specific CI, yes, you can also create a problem ticket.

Why should the change management team have access to the knowledge base? Or Why should the change management interface with knowledge management?

The Change Management team should have access to KB or Change Management should interface with knowledge management because:

- Lessons learned from successful/failed changes should be logged in KB, and this will be done through knowledge management process.
- While handling changes, the change management staff can refer the KB articles (and these knowledge base articles are developed through knowledge management process).

How would you control unauthorized changes in your environment?

Firstly, educate about the process through training sessions and exams for stakeholders (and bring awareness on its importance)

If at first it is not working (Second), define a metric called 'unauthorized changes implemented by an implementer' and highlight the unauthorized changes and its implementers to the management.

Even if this is not working (third), ensure only very designated people (change implementation team) have access privileges to make changes in production environment.

How would you identify unauthorized changes in the IT infrastructure?

The best option to identify unauthorized changes would be to have an automated CMDB and discovery tool which would identify the number newly discovered CIs, modified CIs, deleted CIs in the infrastructure. And accordingly we could check the number of changes implemented with respect to those CIs.

If there is no automated CMDB and discovery tool, then configuration manager has to conduct audits on CIs on a weekly basis to identify the changes that have happened in a week.

What are the challenges that you have faced as a change manager?

Ensuring all the operational teams are following change management process like:

- Technical teams are implementing the change tasks as per planned date and time.
- Technical teams are closing the change tasks after implementation.
- Ensuring the technical teams is updating complete information in the change tasks as per the defined quality parameters.
- Controlling the number of emergency changes.

How would you determine if a change request is really an emergency change request?

If the emergency change request has appropriate business justifications like a major incident, a security concern, any issue that has big financial value associated then it can be characterized as emergency change request.

How often do you have CAB meetings?

Generally, in all companies, CAB meetings happen once or twice in a week. Change requests that need approvals are consolidated with respect to a period of time (like weekly or for three days) and the CAB meetings are organized to do the necessary approvals.

Can change requests be raised proactively?

Yes, change requests can be raised proactively and reactively.

Proactive change requests are those changes which are raised proactively by identifying the alerts/events (which would impact the IT service) from monitoring tools.

Reactive change requests are those changes that are raised to restore/resolve a specific issue.

Appendix

Acronyms

BIA – Business Impact Analysis

CAB – Change Advisory Board

CI – Configuration Item

CMDB – Configuration Management Database

CMS – Configuration Management System

CSF – Critical Success Factors

CSI – Continual Service Improvement

DFSS – Design for Six Sigma

DMAIC – Define, Measure, Analyze, Improve and Control

DMADV – Define, Measure, Analyze, Design and Validate

FSC - Forward Schedule of Changes

KPI – Key Performance Indicators

ITSM – Information Technology Service Management

RACI – Roles, Accountability, Consulted, and Informed

RFC – Request for Change

RFC-FNR – Request for Change for New Requirements

RFC-FRI – Request for Change for Resolving Incidents

RFC-FRO – Request For Change for Routine Operations

RCA – Root Cause Analysis

IMIS – Incident Management Information System

IM – Incident Management

OLA – Operational Level Agreement

PM – Problem Management

SACM – Service Asset and Configuration Management

SLA – Service Level Agreement

SLM – Service Level Management

SLT – Service Level Targets

SOP – Standard Operating Procedures

SPOC – Single Point of Contact

KB – Knowledge Base

KEDB – Known Error Database

UC – Underpinning Contracts

VBF – Vital Business Function

Index

Made in United States
Orlando, FL
11 November 2026

90609397R00095